SUPERMAN
RETURNS

Screenplay by Michael Dougherty & Dan Harris
Story by Bryan Singer & Michael Dougherty & Dan Harris
Superman created by Jerry Siegel and Joe Shuster

LEVEL 3

SCHOLASTIC

Adapted by: Jane Revell
Fact Files written by: Jacquie Bloese
Commissioning Editor: Jacquie Bloese
Editor: Patricia Reilly
Designer: Dawn Wilson
Picture research: Emma Bree
Photo credits:
Cover and inside images courtesy of Warner Bros.
Page 59: Y. Tsuno, V. Bucci/AFP/Getty Images.
Illustrations (page 34): Oxford Illustrators

SUPERMAN, the DC Logo, and all related characters and elements are trademarks of DC Comics © 2006.

All rights reserved.

Published by Scholastic Ltd. 2006

No part of this publication may be reproduced in whole or in part, or stored in a retrieval system, or transmitted in any form or by any means, electronic, mechanical, photocopying, recording or otherwise, without written permission of the publisher. For information regarding permission write to:

Mary Glasgow Magazines (Scholastic Ltd.)
Euston House
24 Eversholt Street
London
NW1 1DB

Printed in Singapore. Reprinted in 2008.
This edition printed in 2009.

Contents

	Page
Superman Returns	**4–55**
People and places	**4**
Chapter 1: New beginnings	6
Chapter 2: Back home	11
Chapter 3: A trip to the Arctic	14
Chapter 4: Clark gets a surprise	17
Chapter 5: Luthor's plan	20
Chapter 6: 'Write about Superman!'	25
Chapter 7: Superman is back!	27
Chapter 8: The robbery	30
Chapter 9: An interview with Superman	34
Chapter 10: Lois investigates	38
Chapter 11: The earthquake	44
Chapter 12: 'Goodbye Superman!'	49
Chapter 13: Superman saves the world	53
Fact Files	**56–61**
Superman: the facts	56
The science of Superman	57
Earthquakes	58
21st century news	60
Self-Study Activities	**62–64**

PEOPLE AND PLACES

SUPERMAN
Superman was born on another planet, Krypton, and came to Earth when he was a baby. He is very strong and he can fly and move very fast. For years he has used his special powers to help people. Only one thing can kill him: kryptonite.

CLARK KENT
Clark Kent is Superman's name when he is an 'ordinary' person. He works as a reporter for a newspaper, the *Daily Planet*. The only person who knows his secret is Martha Kent, his Earth mother.

LEX LUTHOR
Luthor is a very rich businessman. He hates Superman and wants to kill him. He wants to control the world. Kitty Kowalski is his girlfriend. Grant, Riley, Stanford and Brutus work for him.

LOIS LANE

Lois is the woman who Superman/Clark Kent loves. She is a reporter for the *Daily Planet*. She is in love with Superman but she isn't in love with Clark Kent! She lives with Richard White, another reporter. Their son, Jason, is five years old.

PERRY WHITE

Perry White is head of the *Daily Planet*. He is Clark, Lois and Jimmy's boss.

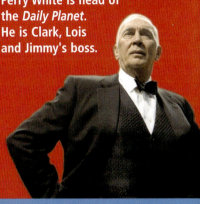

JIMMY OLSEN

Jimmy Olsen is a photographer for the *Daily Planet*. His dream is to take a good photograph of Superman!

PLACES

Metropolis: The city on Earth where Clark Kent lives.

The Daily Planet offices: The home of the newspaper. Clark, Lois, Jimmy, Richard White and Perry work here.

The Fortress of Solitude: A secret place in the Arctic. Superman keeps a special crystal here. He goes here to learn from his father, Jor-El.

Krypton: the planet where Superman was born. It was destroyed by a huge explosion.

The *Gertrude*: Lex Luthor's yacht.

CHAPTER 1
New beginnings

BOOM! An earthquake shook the planet Krypton.

Jor-El and his wife, Lara, stood looking at their baby son, Kal-El.

'Quick, Lara! Soon Krypton will be destroyed!' the man said, 'We must save our son. We must send him to the planet Earth. He will find a new home and be safe.'

'Why Earth, Jor-El?' asked Lara. 'He will be different from everyone there. Life will be very difficult for him.'

'The sun will help him,' Jor-El replied. 'It will help him to fly and to move fast. It will help to protect him.'

'He will be all alone,' Lara said.

Jor-El put the baby on a little bed, in a spaceship made of crystal. 'He will not be alone. He will never be alone,' he said.

He showed Lara a large crystal. Then he put the crystal on the bed next to the baby and closed the spaceship door.

The spaceship carried the baby far into space. 'Sleep my little Kal-El,' his father's voice whispered from the crystal. 'This crystal contains everything I have learned, everything I feel for you. You will travel far, but we will never leave you.'

And while Kal-El slept, Krypton exploded behind him.

❖❖❖

And so Superman grew up on Earth. His name was Clark Kent. He tried to lead a normal life as a reporter for a newspaper. But, it wasn't easy for him because he was also secretly Superman, protector of the world. He felt different from everyone else and he felt alone. He hated lying and living a false life. He couldn't even tell Lois Lane, the woman who he loved. He wanted to tell her the truth, but that was impossible.

Then one day, there was a message from space. It seemed to be a call for help from the destroyed planet Krypton. Superman decided to go back to Krypton. He wanted to help and he also wanted to understand who and what he was. He only told one person he was going away: his Earth mother, Martha Kent. He thought that he would only be away for a few months.

He flew towards the sun to get warmth and light. He had to be strong for his journey to Krypton. Then he climbed into his crystal spaceship and left the Earth. The spaceship was programmed to wake him when he arrived. Once again he slept as he travelled through space.

Superman was dreaming of Krypton when the computer woke him. He felt strange. Where was he?

Suddenly he remembered. 'Krypton,' he whispered excitedly. 'At last.' He flew closer. He looked and listened. He saw that only parts of the planet remained. They were glowing with a scary green light. In the explosion, the crystals of his planet had become kryptonite. Kryptonite could kill Superman.

He felt very ill. His body hurt everywhere.

'Out!' he shouted at his spaceship. 'Away!'

The spaceship moved away from the planet.

'How long have I been away from Earth?' he wondered.

'Time information!' he said to the spaceship. The information appeared.

'No! That's impossible!' he thought. He hadn't been away for months. He'd been away for *years*.

Suddenly something big hit the spaceship. Quickly he looked out of the window. He had flown into a kryptonite storm! He fell on the floor, holding his stomach.

'Earth!' he whispered with difficulty. 'Return to Earth! … Home!'

'Alien!' Martha Kent said. She looked up from the game

of Scrabble.* 'That's … seventy four. Now I've got 409 and you've got 280.'

She stopped suddenly. She heard a strange sound. 'I know that sound,' she thought. 'Clark!'

WHAM! A crash shook the house.

'What was that?!' shouted Ben Hubbard. He quickly picked up the phone. 'We need to call the police!'

'It´s nothing serious, Ben. It's just a meteorite. They sometimes land here,' said Martha. She took the phone from him. 'Listen, it's late. Thanks for dinner. I'll see you tomorrow evening.'

She walked to the door with him. He got into his truck and drove off. Then she quickly put on her jacket, climbed into her truck and drove off.

When she saw a large hole in the road, she stopped and got out. With her lamp she could see small pieces of broken crystal. She walked into the field … and there was the crystal spaceship.

'Clark!' she called. 'Son!'

'Mom,' he whispered. And he fell into her arms.

* Scrabble is a board game. You use the letters to make words.

In a very big house in a rich part of the city of Metropolis, an old woman was dying. She smiled at the blond man who was sitting next to her bed.

'I know you're a good man,' she said. 'When I helped you to get out of prison you promised to take care of me. And you *have* taken care of me.'

The blond man smiled and gave her a large piece of paper. He put a pen in her hand.

'That's why I'm going to give you everything,' the old woman continued.

She started to write her name on the paper: *Gertrude Vander* ... Her eyes closed and she died.

'No!' the man thought. 'Not now! Not when I'm so near!'

He took her hand and finished writing her name: *Gertrude Vanderworth*. He took the paper and opened the bedroom door. The woman's son and his family were waiting. The man took the blond wig from his head and threw it at the woman's son.

'You can keep that!' Lex Luthor laughed as he walked towards the front door. 'Everything else is mine.'

CHAPTER 2
Back home

Clark opened his eyes. He was in bed at home. The old dog was beside his bed. 'Hey, boy,' he said. 'Need to go outside?'

'Five years,' thought Clark. 'I've been away for five whole years!'

He looked around the farm. The vehicles were broken, the fields were empty … Things were terrible. The dog put its head in Clark's hand, Clark suddenly remembered his twelfth birthday, the day he got the dog …

He was running through the field with the little dog. Then, amazingly, he was flying. Up and up and up. As he was flying down again, Clark found he could see under the ground. In one of the farm buildings there was a small room with something like a very large egg in it. Clark went into the room. He touched the egg and it opened. Inside there was a large crystal. Clark picked it up and it shone with light. That was the day Clark began to understand that he was different. He was special. And he was alone.

In a corner of a farm building Clark found a lot of old *Daily Planet* newspapers. He looked at some of the headlines: SIGNAL FROM DESTROYED PLANET: IS THERE LIFE ON KRYPTON? Then, SUPERMAN DISAPPEARS. And later WHERE HAS HE GONE? and WILL HE EVER RETURN?

And then, several months ago, there was an article by Lois Lane: WHY THE WORLD DOESN'T NEED SUPERMAN.

'The world has been waiting for Superman's return for five long years,' the article began.

Clark read quickly until he reached the final few lines.

'People have always wanted gods and super heroes to fly down from the sky and help them with their problems. But in the end, these super heroes always leave and the problems are still there.

We wait for the super hero to return, but he never does. And finally we understand that life would be better if he hadn't come at all.'

That night, Clark sat at the kitchen table. The evening news programmes were on the TV.

'A bank in Chicago was robbed today …'

Clark changed the programme. Click!

'A gas explosion in Baltimore …'

Click!

'A fire in an office building …'

Click!

'Train passengers were attacked by gunmen …'

'I know I can't stop all these bad things, but I tried to help people,' Clark thought to himself. 'But perhaps Lois is right. If people didn't depend on me, they would do something about their own problems. The world would be better without me.'

'Feeling better?' asked his mom as she came into the room.

Clark looked up and saw that she was crying.

'What is it, Mom?' he said.

Martha smiled. 'You were away for so long, I was frightened … Did you find your home?'

'This is my home,' he said.

Martha sat down at the table and took Clark's hands.

'When are you going to Metropolis?' she asked.

'I thought I'd stay here and work on the farm. There's a lot to do.'

'What about that girl you used to like – Lois Lane?'

'It's been five years …'

'Why don't you work for the *Daily Planet* again? They need good reporters.'

There was a knock at the door and a man looked in.

Martha smiled. 'Ben. Come in.'

Ben gave Martha some flowers and kissed her.

'Ben, this is my son, Clark,' Martha said. 'Ben and I are going out to dinner to celebrate, Clark. We're getting married.'

'Getting married!' said Clark in surprise.

'I'll wait in the truck,' said Ben. He went out.

Martha took Clark's hand. 'Listen,' she said, 'I loved your father, Clark, he was very special. But he died a long time ago and now I'm ready for a new life. I'm selling the farm and Ben and I are moving to Montana.' She kissed him. 'We'll talk more tomorrow,' she said.

CHAPTER 3
A trip to the Arctic

The beautiful yacht, *Gertrude*, was moving through the ice in the Arctic Ocean. The yacht had everything: a swimming-pool, a grand piano, a games room, amazing bedrooms, a wonderful kitchen … even a place for a helicopter to land.

Lex Luthor was sitting on the beautiful sofa in the 'living room' with his friend, Kitty Kowalski, a dark-haired attractive woman.

'Yes, this yacht is fantastic,' he thought, 'and it's *my* yacht now.'

There was a knock at the door and two men, Grant and Riley, came in.

'We've found it!' they said.

Luthor smiled. 'Perfect,' he said. 'Stop the yacht.'

They flew several kilometers in the helicopter and then walked through the ice and snow: Luthor, Kitty, Grant, Riley, and two other men, Stanford and Brutus. It was cold and horrible.

'What *are* we doing here?' asked Kitty.

'Do you know the story of Prometheus?' Luthor asked.

'Who?'

'Prometheus. He was a god who stole fire from the other gods and gave it to ordinary people.'

'We're here to steal fire? In the Arctic?'

'More or less,' said Luthor. 'When Prometheus gave us fire, he gave us technology. That's what we're here for.'

Suddenly there was a building in front of them.

'What's this? It's like a huge church made of ice!' said Kitty.

'Not ice, crystal,' said Luthor.

They walked in.

'Was this Superman's house?' whispered Riley. He was carrying a camcorder. He started filming.

'No,' said Luthor. 'But it's very important. It has technology from Superman's world.'

Suddenly, Kitty looked at Luthor. 'Why *did* Superman leave?' she said. 'Did you have anything to do with it?'

'Well, let's say … we helped him decide,' laughed Luthor.

In the centre of the main room was a large machine with lots of crystals on top of it. Luthor touched a crystal. Immediately, the machine began to shine. All the crystals moved. The large crystal in the centre shone brilliantly.

A picture of a man with white hair appeared all over the walls.

'My son!' he said. 'I have taught you many things for many years. What questions do you have for me now?'

'Oh!' whispered Kitty, 'Superman's father! Can he see us?'

'No, it's just a film,' said Luthor, 'but it thinks I'm Superman, so it's going to help me.'

He smiled. 'Tell me everything about crystals,' he said.

CHAPTER 4
Clark gets a surprise

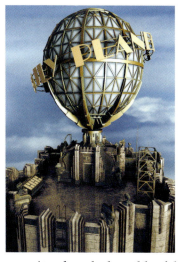

Clark walked into the Daily Planet building with his bags and went to meet his old boss, Perry White. He felt very lucky that Perry had given him a job again. After all, he had left very suddenly five years ago.

He walked through the main newspaper room. It was crowded with desks and chairs, computers, telephones and newspapers. He looked for Lois. She wasn't at her desk and he felt sad. His bag hit someone's desk and a camera began to fall. Superman caught it super fast before it broke on the floor.

'Hey! Careful!' said a voice behind him. Clark turned round. It was Jimmy Olsen, a photographer.

'Mr Clark! I mean Kent. Mr Kent,' Jimmy said excitedly. 'Oh, wow! Welcome back!'

He ran off and came back with a cake. 'I made this for you myself,' he said.

'Thanks, Jimmy!' said Clark.

'It's good that someone's happy to see me,' he thought.

Perry White came out of his office.

'Hey boss, look who's here!' shouted Jimmy.

White came over and shook hands with Clark.

'Thanks for giving me my job back, boss,' said Clark.

He picked up his bags and began to walk towards his

old desk next to Lois's.

'Not over there, Mr Kent!' said Jimmy, 'This way.' Jimmy walked to a small desk in the corner. 'You've got Jack Green's old desk. See you later.' He walked away.

There was a small room behind the desk. Clark carried his bags into the room, shut the door and opened one of them. Inside was a photo of his parents. Under the photo were his red and blue Superman clothes. He shut the bag again and hid it behind a cupboard.

Then he heard Jimmy's voice: 'Mr Kent! Where are you? Look – Lois is on television!'

Jimmy was watching a news programme which showed reporters on a special plane. On top of the plane was the NASA* rocket *Explorer*. The rocket would be launched from the plane in the sky. At the front of the plane was the woman from NASA, Bobbie-Faye.

'This is a very exciting moment,' she was saying.

Lois's hand went up. 'Lois Lane, *Daily Planet*,' she said. 'This new test is costing millions of dollars, isn't it?' she asked.

Bobbie-Faye looked angrily at Lois. 'I'll answer that question later,' she said.

Clark walked over to Lois's desk. It was full of papers and old coffee cups. He smiled and thought, 'Some things don't change.'

There was an invitation to the Pulitzer Prize Awards*. Lois had won the award for her article: WHY THE WORLD DOESN'T NEED SUPERMAN.

'It's the right decision to stop being Superman,' he thought.

Then Clark saw a photo of Lois standing next to a

---

* NASA is the National Aeronautics and Space Administration.
* Pulitzer Prizes are awards given to reporters in America for excellent articles.

handsome man with dark hair. They were holding the hands of a small boy. Who was the man? Who was the boy?

Then he saw a child's drawing of a house with the words TO MOM at the top, and the name JASON at the bottom.

Clark looked at the photo again. 'He looks like his mother, doesn't he?' said Jimmy behind him.

'His … mother?' said Clark.

'Yes, he's Lois's son,' said Jimmy. 'I thought you knew.'

'Is Lois married?' asked Clark.

'Not exactly,' said Jimmy. 'Are you OK, Clark? Listen, let's go and have some lunch.'

When they got to the restaurant, the television was still showing the plane.

'When we get to 13,350 metres, the rocket will take off and leave the plane behind,' Bobbie-Faye was saying.

Lois asked another question.

Clark felt sad. 'I know things change,' he said, 'but I never thought Lois would …'

'*I* think she's still in love with Superman,' said Jimmy.

CHAPTER 5
Luthor's plan

Lex Luthor opened the front door of Gertrude Vanderworth's house and went in. The others followed. They went downstairs into a big dark room. Luthor took the large Kryptonian crystal out of his pocket.

'If this crystal has water, it will grow,' he said.

He turned on the lights. On tables all around the room was a model of the city of Metropolis.

'Wow!' said Grant. 'It's Metropolis. Roads, buildings … Look! The trains are moving.'

'And there are boats on the rivers!' said Kitty. 'They're moving too. And there's the house we're in now.'

Stanford was looking at the crystal carefully. Finally he cut off a very small piece.

'Are you filming this, Riley?' said Luthor. Riley turned on his camcorder. Stanford carried the piece of crystal to the model of Metropolis. He put it into the sea. Nothing happened. Then suddenly all the trains began to slow. And the lights in the Vanderworth house went out.

Across the city there was a blackout. The lights went out in the restaurant where Clark and Jimmy were eating. Clark looked through the wall into the street. The traffic wasn't moving.

'That's very strange,' he thought. 'I wonder what's happening.'

In the plane, high above the Atlantic, the lights also went out … and the engines stopped. The plane began to drop.

'We're going down,' thought Lois. 'We're going to crash!'

Then suddenly the engines started again and the lights came on. But Lois knew there was a big problem. 'They will have to stop the test,' she thought.

The lights came on again in the restaurant where Clark and Jimmy were eating. And across Metropolis, buses, cars and trains began to move. Metropolis was alive again.

The lights came on too in the downstairs room in the Vanderworth house.

'Is that it?' asked Kitty.

'No,' said Luthor. 'Just wait. Keep filming, Riley.'

Suddenly the model of Metropolis began to shake. Trains crashed, buildings fell down … The walls in the room shook, the water pipes broke and water exploded everywhere. And as they watched, the piece of crystal in the water began to grow.

'Amazing,' said Luthor. 'Completely amazing.'

On the plane, Lois heard the countdown (10, 9, 8 …) and the pilot's voice calling NASA: 'We are going to stop the test. Hello? Can you hear me?'

'Yes, we can hear you,' said NASA. 'Free the rocket.'

(5, 4, 3 …) 'I'm trying, but I can't,' said the pilot. 'Can you free the rocket from there?'

'No, it's impossible,' said NASA.

(2, 1 …) BOOM!

The plane jumped forward with a loud noise and some passengers were thrown to the floor.

'Oh no!' thought Lois. 'We're still joined to the rocket. We're going to crash.' She thought about her son at school and hoped he wasn't watching the television. She didn't want him to see her die.

The news travelled around the world. The rocket *Explorer* was in serious trouble. It was still joined to the plane and they would both probably crash.

In the restaurant, Jimmy watched the terrible news.

'Clark!' he shouted. 'Lois is on that plane.'

He looked across the table. But Clark had gone. Clark was running super fast down the street to the Daily Planet building. After reading Lois's article, he didn't want to be Superman anymore, but it was no good. His Earth father had once told him that he was on Earth for a reason. He knew his father was right. He had to save those people.

He ran into the building and flew up to the eighteenth floor. In the small room behind his desk he took off his glasses, pulled on his red and blue clothes and ran to an open window.

Then VOOSH! He was flying up and up. Superman had returned.

Up ahead, the rocket *Explorer* was flying fast towards space, taking the plane with it.

Under the rocket, the plane shook terribly. 'It's not strong enough,' Lois thought. 'It's going to break into pieces.' She didn't want to think about dying.

She looked out of the window and saw the stars. Beautiful. And she thought about *him*.

Five years ago, Superman had disappeared. People said he had gone to live in the stars. Lois wished …

Something red and blue flew past the window. It looked like … No, it couldn't be. That was impossible.

Superman landed on top of the plane. He put his body between the plane and the rocket and pushed as hard as he could. Finally the rocket broke away from the plane. Superman took it in both hands and threw it into space.

'Just like playing with a paper plane,' he thought.

Then he flew down past the falling plane. Below he saw a baseball stadium full of people. Everyone was screaming and trying to escape.

Superman got under the front of the plane and pushed it up with his hands. The plane slowed and then stopped.

Superman put it down carefully on the field. He could hear people saying: 'It's Superman! He's back! Superman has returned!'
Superman pulled off the door and went into the plane. 'Is everyone okay?' he asked. Everyone said yes. 'Are *you* okay?' he asked Lois. Lois made a noise. Superman smiled.

He turned and left the plane. Lois ran to the door and watched him fly up into the sky.

Luthor looked at the model of Metropolis. The crystal had grown up through the city and destroyed it.

'Did you film everything?' he asked Riley.

'Yes, I got it all. It was scary,' said Riley.

CHAPTER 6
'Write about Superman!'

Perry White was angry. 'I want to know everything,' he said.

He looked at Jimmy. 'I want some amazing photos of Superman. Flying into the stadium ... leaving the stadium ... anything.'

He looked at the sports reporter. 'I want to know how this will change baseball games. How will they get the plane out of the stadium?'

He looked at the travel reporter. 'Find out where he went for five years. Was he on holiday? If he was, where did he go?'

He looked at Lois. 'Remember this story isn't about the blackout, Lois. It's about Superman!'

'No, it isn't, boss.' said Lois. 'The blackout is the really important story here. It wasn't just the lights that went out. Everything stopped. Everything!'

'Listen to me, Lois.' said White. 'There are three things that sell newspapers: deaths, people's secrets and Superman ... so you're going to write about Superman!'

The meeting was over and Clark sat at his desk.

'Hi,' said a voice. 'Who are you?'

Clark looked and saw the boy from Lois's photo standing there. He was about four or five, thin, with glasses and thick brown hair.

'Hello,' said Clark. 'I'm Clark. An old friend ... of your

mom's. From before you were born.'

'Really?' said the boy. 'She's never talked about you.'

Clark felt sad.

'Jason!' shouted Lois. She ran over and picked him up. Then she saw Clark.

'Hello, Clark,' she said. 'Welcome back. I see you've met my son.'

'I saw you on TV, Lois,' said Clark. 'Are you OK?'

'Oh that was nothing,' she said.

'Oh, and I heard about your Pulitzer award. Well done.'

'Yes, can you believe it?' she said.

The man from the photo walked over.

'Hi, Daddy!' shouted Jason.

Lois kissed the man. Clark felt uncomfortable. He coughed.

'Oh!' Lois turned to Clark. 'Clark, this is Richard White. He works on international news and he's a pilot. Richard, this is Clark Kent.'

'Great to meet you, Clark,' said Richard.

'I've got to go,' said Lois. 'I've got a story to write.'

'About Superman?' asked Richard.

'No,' said Lois. 'About the blackout. I'm going to find out what happened. Bye. See you later!'

CHAPTER 7
Superman is back!

Luthor picked up the morning newspaper. On the front page, there was a photograph of Superman looking very handsome. SUPERMAN IS BACK the headline said.

Kitty looked at the photograph too. 'Hell-o, handsome!' she said.

Luthor looked angry. He threw the newspaper on the ground. On the back was a headline: WORLD'S LARGEST COLLECTION OF METEORITES AT METROPOLIS MUSEUM

Grant, Riley, Stanford and Brutus arrived in the truck.

'We've got it, boss,' Grant said. He showed Luthor a large, long box.

'Put it on the yacht,' said Luthor.

Brutus and Grant carried the box onto the yacht. The others followed.

'What are we going to do about Superman, boss?' asked Stanford. He was worried.

'We thought he would *die* up there on Krypton,' Stanford said. 'But now he's back. He'll find out how we sent false messages and tricked him. He's not stupid. He'll find us!'

'You worry too much, Stanford,' said Luthor.

Brutus opened the box. Inside was a rocket launcher.

Clark and Lois left the building together after work and walked along the street. Clark was worried about her. She was thinner and she looked unhappy.

'How's your first week back at work?' she asked him.

'It's OK,' he said. 'Do you want to …?'

'Can I ask you something?' she said quickly. 'Have you ever been in love? Or met someone completely different from you but completely right for you? But then he disappears and doesn't even say goodbye?'

'Perhaps he had to go,' said Clark. 'Maybe he was frightened to say goodbye. Maybe he thought if he saw you again, he wouldn't be able to leave you. Who are we talking about?'

'Nobody,' said Lois. 'Forget it. TAXI!'

'Do you want to have dinner?' asked Clark.

'I'd love to,' she said, 'but I have to get home.'

A taxi stopped and Lois got in.

'312 Riverside Drive,' she told the driver. 'Bye, Clark.'

'See you, Lois,' he said.

Soon after, Superman flew over Metropolis. People looked up and pointed and shouted excitedly, 'It's Superman! See? He *is* back!'

Superman was looking for Riverside Drive. Number 312.

He found it. Richard's seaplane was on the river outside and there were toys in the garden. Superman's eyes could see inside the house too. Jason's room upstairs was full of model planes and toy trains. His parents' room had books, magazines and clothes everywhere.

Lois was in the kitchen and Richard was putting plates on the table. Jason was playing the piano.

'You're not eating or sleeping, Lois,' said Richard. 'Is something wrong?'

'Wrong …?'

'I promised I would never ask you this, but now that he's back … were you in love with him?'

Lois smiled. She started to put the food on the plates. 'He was Superman. Everyone was in love with him.'

'But were you?'

'No,' she said. 'I wasn't!'

Superman's heart was heavy. 'She told Richard she didn't love me, but I'm sure she did.'

He flew up and away from the house.

'I can't be with Lois,' he thought. 'She has a life without me and she has a son.'

And he remembered his father Jor-El's words: 'Even though you have grown up on Earth, you are not one of them.'

'I have no right to have a normal life. If I had a normal life, I would have to lie. I could never tell anyone that Clark Kent was Superman,' he thought.

'I am different and special. I am here for a reason. I must use all that I have learned to help people.'

He flew down to Metropolis.

CHAPTER 8
The robbery

Superman flew above the city, looking for trouble. He saw a car driving fast towards a crowd of people. The dark-haired woman inside was trying to stop the car but she couldn't. She was screaming.

Superman landed in front of the car and picked up the front. 'Turn off the engine!' he shouted.

He put the car down and went around to the driver's door. 'Are you okay, Miss?' he asked.

Kitty Kowalski got out of the car. She was wearing an expensive black dress.

'My heart!' she whispered and fell into Superman's arms. Superman picked her up and flew to Metropolis General Hospital.

It was ten minutes before closing time at the Metropolitan Museum of Natural History when Luthor and his men arrived. They were dressed as tourists.

In one of the rooms Luthor found what he was looking for. It was an ugly brown meteorite, the size of a football. When he pulled it from the wall, several guards came running in. Grant and Brutus hit them on the head and they fell to the floor.

Riley filmed as Luthor carefully cut off the outside of the meteorite. Inside the meteorite shone a scary green light. Kryptonite!

Superman landed with Kitty outside the Metropolis General Hospital.

Kitty looked quickly at her watch. 'Luthor needs just a little more time,' she thought.

She smiled at Superman. 'Thank you, Superman. My heart is better. You're wonderful. What did you do?'

'Nothing,' said Superman. 'But I must …'

'Please call me Katherine,' she said.

'I really must go, Katherine.'

'Would you like to have a coffee?' she said. 'No, you've got too much to do. Places to go. People to save. Thanks for your help. Bye.'

Kitty turned and walked away. Superman watched her go. 'She doesn't *look* ill,' he thought.

Then he flew up into the sky.

During the next eighteen hours, Superman seemed to be everywhere. In Germany, he caught two window cleaners before they fell to their deaths. In Africa, he stopped a plane from crashing. It was carrying food for hungry people. He saved one ship in a storm and stopped a fire on another ship. There were stories about him in newspapers and on television all around the world.

'All those people have pictures of Superman,' said Jimmy Olsen, 'and I have nothing!'

Clark walked into the newspaper building smiling happily. He'd had a very good lunchtime: he had rescued a cat from a tree, saved some fishermen who had fallen into the sea and stopped a fire near Los Angeles.

Now it was time to meet in Perry's office. When he arrived, Lois was already there. She was looking at the words SUPER SAVE! on the front page of another newspaper. There was a photo of Superman with Kitty Kowalski in his arms.

'That photo was taken by a twelve-year old with a camera phone,' said Perry. 'What have you got, Olsen?'

Jimmy was silent.

'And I don't know what you've been doing, Lois,' Perry said. 'Other reporters have got Superman stories and they don't even know him. You do.'

'But there are more important stories, Perry,' said Lois. 'Like the museum robbery last night.'

'A robbery at the museum?' thought Clark. 'When was that?'

'Even Superman missed it,' Lois continued. 'He was too busy saving that … that woman.'

'And what did they steal?' asked Perry.

'A meteorite,' said Lois.

'That's boring,' said Perry.

'What about the blackout?' said Lois.

'Kent can do the blackout story,' said Perry. 'I want you to do Superman, Lois. Super. Man. OK?'

'OK,' said Lois and she left the room. Clark followed her.

'I'm sorry, Lois,' he said.

She took the papers that were on her desk and put them in a box that said BLACKOUT. 'Take these,' she said.

Richard came into the office and saw the BLACKOUT box that Clark was carrying.

'I thought you were doing that story, Lois,' he said.

'I've got to do Superman,' she said. 'I'm so angry.'

'I've got an idea,' said Richard, 'I'll help with Superman, and you and Clark can work on the blackout together.'

'That would be great,' said Lois.

Clark smiled. 'That's a good idea,' he said.

Kitty walked onto the yacht and hit Luthor in the face.

'I was going to pretend that my brakes weren't working. *Pretend*!' she shouted. 'You didn't have to cut them!'

'Of course I did,' said Luthor. 'Superman knows if someone is pretending. He can see inside people and things, remember?!'

Kitty was still angry. 'Did you get your meteorite?' she asked.

'Yes, I did.' He pointed to a map on the wall with lots of pins. It showed Metropolis and the Atlantic Ocean.

'And this,' he said, pointing to the largest pin, 'is where we're going.'

'I'm going to start, Mr Luthor,' shouted Stanford from outside. Luthor went out.

Stanford had cut off the outside of the meteorite. Only the shining green part was left.

'Do it,' said Luthor.

Stanford began to cut small pieces off the green meteorite. They were long and pointed, like sharp knives. Luthor picked up the largest piece and put it in his pocket.

CHAPTER 9
An interview with Superman

'What's wrong, Jimmy?' asked Clark.

'I've been trying all week to get a good photo of Superman, but he moves too fast.'

'Keep trying,' said Clark. 'You'll get one some day.'

Jason ran past making a strange noise and crashed into a desk.

'Is Jason OK, Jimmy?' Clark asked.

'I think so,' said Jimmy. 'Miss Lane doesn't like to talk about it, but it seems he had a few health problems when he was born.'

Lois was looking at a large map of Metropolis and the Atlantic Ocean. She circled one place and wrote a number beside it.

'If these times are correct, it looks like the blackout started in just one place,' she said.

Richard was reading about Superman on Lois's computer. He looked up.

'Does Superman hear each sound by itself or does he hear everything all together?' he asked.

'Both,' said Lois.

'He's very tall,' said Richard, 'and he can see through anything. That would be fun.'

'He weighs 225 pounds,' said Lois, 'he can move super fast, he never lies and the only thing that can kill him is kryptonite.'

'Jason,' shouted Richard. 'Let's go and get some food for everyone. Do you want to come, Jimmy?'

Clark looked at Lois. Now that they were alone, he wanted to say something. But what?

'You know, Lois … I wanted to ask you about that article …'

Lois stood up suddenly. 'I need to go outside for a moment,' she said. 'Let's talk when I get back.'

Lois went to the top of the newspaper building. It was getting dark.

'Hello,' said a voice.

Lois jumped and looked up. Superman was just above her.

'I didn't mean to frighten you,' he said. 'I'm here for an interview!'

'Really?' she said, surprised. She looked for her tape recorder.

'It's in your coat pocket,' said Superman.

She smiled. Superman always knew where things were. She turned on the recorder.

'Let's start with the big question,' she said. 'Where did you go?'

'To Krypton.'

'But you told me it was destroyed.'

'It was. But five years ago there was a message from there, so I wanted to be sure.'

'And what did you find?'

'Nothing, the planet was destroyed. In the explosion, the pieces of the planet became kryptonite. It made me very ill. I almost didn't come back again.'

'Well, you are back,' said Lois, 'and everyone seems happy about it.'

'Not everyone,' said Superman. 'I read your article, Lois: WHY THE WORLD DOESN'T NEED SUPERMAN. Why did you write it?'

Lois turned off the recorder. 'Why did you leave me like that?' she asked him. 'A guy at work says it's because it was too difficult to say goodbye.'

'Maybe he's right. I'm sorry,' said Superman. He held out his hand. 'Come with me. There's something I want to show you. Please.'

They flew up and up and up, high above Metropolis.

'What can you hear?' asked Superman.

'Nothing,' she said. 'It's quiet.'

'I can hear everything,' said Superman. 'I can hear people everywhere crying for help. They need me, Lois.'

They flew back to the top of the Daily Planet building.

Lois looked into Superman's eyes. Their faces were very close.

Suddenly she jumped back.

'Richard is a good man,' she said, 'and you've been away a long time.'

'I know.'

Lois walked towards the door. 'Will I see you around?'

she asked.

'I'm always around,' he said. 'Good night, Lois.'

'Food!'

Richard, Jason and Jimmy came through the door carrying paper bags.

Clark looked up from the papers on his desk. He wasn't really reading. He was thinking about Lois. She had written that article, in part, because he had left her, but her life had changed since then. Now Clark's life had to change too.

'Where's Lois?' said Richard.

Just at that moment, Lois walked in.

'Where have you been?' asked Richard.

Lois seemed half-asleep. 'Oh,' she said. 'Just on the roof … getting some air.'

Lois threw her article onto Perry's desk.

'An interview with Superman? Is this real?' he asked.

'Yes, it's real,' said Lois.

'How did you find him?'

'He found me,' she said, 'so now I'd like to do the story about the blackout.'

'Kent's doing the blackout story,' said Perry. 'Have you got a beautiful dress to wear tonight?' he continued. 'This is the biggest night of your life, Lois.'

'It feels a bit strange,' she said, 'I won an award for an article called WHY THE WORLD DOESN'T NEED SUPERMAN. But now I've just written an article saying that we *do* need Superman!'

'You've won a big award, Lois,' said Perry. That's the important thing. Just enjoy tonight.'

CHAPTER 10
Lois investigates

Superman flew to the Arctic Ocean. He hadn't been there for five years, but now he needed to talk to his father. He flew down through the clouds and landed in front of the Fortress of Solitude.

It felt ... dead. Strange. Wrong.

He ran inside. 'Father!' he shouted. No crystals shone. No voice welcomed him.

The large crystal wasn't there. The crystal that had travelled with him to Earth when he was a baby. The centre of Kryptonian life. It had gone.

'I've got your dress, Miss Lane!' Jimmy ran across the office carrying a long blue evening dress in a big plastic bag.

Lois was on the phone. 'Water and Light Department, please. Hello? This is Lois Lane from the Daily Planet. Could I- Yes, Superman is very nice – but could I ask you a few questions about the blackout?'

Jimmy hung up her dress and put a note on her desk: RICHARD'S LATE. CAN YOU PICK UP JASON FROM SCHOOL?

An hour later, Lois was sitting at her desk, wearing the blue evening dress. As she talked on the phone, she was putting on her earrings.

'So the lights went out in West End at 12.36 and City Centre ten seconds later. And before that? Racine and Newtown. Right.'

She wrote numbers on the map.

'And before that? In Hobbs Edge. You're sure?' She

wrote again.

'And nothing before that? Thank you very much.'

She put the phone down and looked at the map. Then she began to draw circles. The centre of all the circles was a house next to the river. She wrote an X on it.

She looked up at the clock. It was 4.30.

'Oh no! Jason!'

She quickly took the map and her bag and ran to the door.

Lois stopped the car in front of Jason's school. Jason was waiting with his teacher.

'You're late, mom,' he said.

'I know, honey. I'm sorry.'

Lois waved to the teacher and drove off.

'Daddy's waiting for us at the office,' said Lois, 'but first we have to make one quick visit.'

They stopped in front of a large house with a swimming-pool.

Lois's phone rang. She saw that it was Richard and left

the phone in the car.

'I'll call him back when we come out,' she told herself.

'Come on, Jason,' she said. 'I just need to ask these people a few questions.'

Nobody came to the front door. Lois and Jason heard music playing somewhere. They followed the sound to the back of the house. It was coming from a yacht on the river, the *Gertrude*. There was nobody around.

'I'll just find out who lives here,' thought Lois.

They walked onto the yacht and up some stairs. Lois tried to open several doors. Finally one door opened. It was a small room full of clothes.

'Look, mom!' said Jason.

Lois turned. Jason was pointing to a box full of wigs.

'Oh no,' she thought. 'Now I know who this yacht belongs to.'

There was the noise of an engine. 'The ship's moving,' Lois thought.

'Quick, Jason!' she said, taking his hand. 'We've got to get out of here.'

Another door opened and a man stood there. 'Lois Lane!' he said. 'How nice to see you again.'

It was Lex Luthor.

Lois and Jason were in the main room with Luthor and the others. Lois looked at Kitty Kowalski.

'That's the woman who Superman rescued the other night,' she thought. 'Luthor is certainly doing something bad.'

'And what's your name?' Luthor asked Jason.

'I don't talk to strangers,' said Jason.

'I'm not really a stranger,' said Luthor. 'We're old friends, aren't we, Lois?'

'I thought you were still in prison,' said Lois.

'I had a little help to get free,' said Luthor.

Then she had another thought. 'Did *you* have anything to do with the blackout, Luthor?' she asked.

Luthor smiled. 'Do you want an interview, Miss Lane?'

'Let's go back and call a taxi for Jason,' said Lois. 'Then you can do anything you want with me.'

'Sorry, Miss Lane,' said Luthor. 'We're going somewhere special.'

It was 6.30pm when Clark walked into the Daily Planet office. Jimmy looked up from his desk. He was white.

'What's wrong, Jimmy?' said Clark.

'Lois and Jason have disappeared,' said Jimmy.

Clark ran to Perry's office. Richard was there with Perry.

'I've just heard the news,' said Clark. 'How can I help?'

'She isn't answering her mobile,' said Perry. 'You're a reporter, Kent. Help Richard find her.'

'What do you know about crystals, Miss Lane?' asked Luthor.

'They're very pretty,' said Lois.

'They grow very fast. They love to grow,' said Luthor. He was holding a large, white crystal. Lois remembered it from somewhere. 'This is a very special crystal,' said Luthor.

He pointed to a map on the wall. 'I'm going to build an island. Here in the sea near Metropolis,' he said, 'and it will grow and grow and grow until it almost reaches Europe. I will call it 'New Krypton!''

'Why?' Lois asked.

'Why? Because people need land and they will pay millions for it,' he said.

Lois got up to study the map more closely. 'But your New Krypton is in a very dangerous place,' she said. 'There will be earthquakes. Thousands of people will die.'

'Millions!' said Luthor. 'I can't help that. It's the best place for the crystal to grow.'

'You're mad, Luthor,' Lois said. 'Superman will never let you …'

'Superman won't be able to stop me,' said Luthor. He opened a metal box. A green light shone out of it.

'Kryptonite!' whispered Lois. She sat down heavily on the sofa.

Jason began to play the piano.

'I think Superman's a lost, little boy looking for a home,' said Luthor. 'That's why he went back to Krypton.' He sat down beside Jason and played the piano with him.

'How do you know he went to find Krypton?' asked Lois. 'He didn't tell anyone. And my article hasn't appeared in the newspaper yet.' She thought for a moment. 'It was you, wasn't it? You made him go.'

Luthor started to play faster and faster. Jason copied him perfectly. Luthor stood up angrily.

'Who's his father?' he asked.

'Richard White.'

'Are you sure?' Luthor said. He took the metal box with the kryptonite and walked over to Jason. He opened it. Nothing happened.

Grant called from outside. 'Latitude 39 degrees north, and longitude 71 degrees west, sir.'

With the box under his arm, Luthor walked to the door.

'Watch them carefully,' he said to Brutus as he left.

Lois quickly wrote down the position of the yacht: 39 deg N, 71 deg W. Now all she had to do was tell the world.

CHAPTER 11
The earthquake

Luthor and Kitty climbed the steps to the top of the yacht. Riley followed them with his camcorder. Grant was already there. He was checking the rocket launcher. Luthor opened the metal box and took out the kryptonite. He took the large crystal out of his pocket and put it inside the kryptonite.

'This is going to be good,' he said.

Brutus was bored. Jason was playing an easy tune on the piano. Brutus sat down next to him.

'It's fun,' said Jason. 'Go on, try it.' Brutus began to play.

Lois quickly wrote 'Help us! Lois Lane' on the paper under '39 deg N, 71 deg W'. She moved quietly to the fax machine and put the paper in. She was going to send the message to the Daily Planet. She pushed 'send'. The paper began to move slowly through the machine.

Luthor put the crystal and kryptonite into the rocket. Riley started filming.

Luthor stepped back. 'Ready!' he said.

BOOM!

The rocket flew through the air and hit the water. Luthor watched it disappear. All the lights went out on the yacht.

Clark, Richard and Jimmy were standing around Lois's desk.

'She was working on a map,' said Jimmy. 'Drawing circles.'

'Where is it?' said Richard.

'She probably took it with her,' said Clark.

'Perhaps she left some notes on her computer,' said Richard. 'What's the password? Let's try – *Jason*. No. *Richard*. No.'

'Try *Superman*,' said Clark.

Richard typed *Superman*. The computer unlocked. Then all the lights went out. Thirty seconds later they came back on. The television gave the amazing news. There had been a blackout across the world.

Luthor was pleased. He imagined the crystal and kryptonite growing under the sea. He checked his watch.

BOOM!

He smiled. The growing crystal was going deeper and deeper. He checked his watch again.

WHROOOM!

There was a huge explosion. The sky and the sea were on fire. Deep under the sea he could see a deadly green light. Crystal mountains began to rise.

Lois looked at the fax machine. Her message hadn't gone. Jason and Brutus were still playing the piano. She took the paper out and put it in again. The message got to HELP US! and then stopped. Lois looked around. Brutus had turned off the machine. He picked up Lois and threw her across the room.

In the Daily Planet office, Jimmy Olsen heard the fax machine. He ran over and read the message. Quickly he put the fax in front of Richard and Clark.

'Call the sea police, Jimmy,' said Richard, 'I'm going to get my seaplane. Are you coming, Clark?'

'No, thanks,' said Clark. 'I don't like flying.'

Superman flew high into the sky. As he flew out to sea, he heard noises under the ocean. He looked down with his special eyes and could see the seabed breaking open. The earthquake was moving fast towards Metropolis. Superman flew back. He wanted to get to the city first.

At the same time, out in the Atlantic, the storm shook Luthor's yacht. Things crashed onto the floor. Brutus moved towards Lois with a large stick.

'Mom! Move!' Jason shouted.

Suddenly the yacht fell to the side. The piano jumped across the floor and hit Brutus, pushing him against the wall.

'Come on, Jason,' shouted Lois. 'You've been really brave. I need you to be brave a little longer.'

She opened the door. Outside were Riley and Grant. Grant had a gun.

'We're going to lock you in the kitchen,' said Grant. 'We leave the ship in three minutes!'

Superman reached Metropolis at the same time as the earthquake. Buildings were shaking and frightened people ran out of shops and restaurants. A mother and her baby daughter screamed as they fell into a huge hole. Then Superman was there, carrying them to safety.

In the Daily Planet building all the lights went out.
'Not another blackout!' shouted Perry White.
The building shook dangerously.
'I don't think *this* is a blackout,' said Jimmy.

Superman tried to be everywhere at once: flying people to safety, carrying people with injuries to hospital, stopping accidents and fires … When two very tall buildings started to fall towards each other, Superman put a large machine between them. He hoped that would give the people inside the buildings time to escape.

The yacht *Gertrude* was beginning to go under the water. As Luthor was putting all his favourite wigs into a bag, he heard Lois shouting angrily, 'Let us out, Luthor.'

He walked past the kitchen window and looked in. He smiled at Lois and waved. Minutes later, his helicopter was in the sky.

Jimmy, Perry and many other people ran from office buildings in the city centre. The huge globe on top of the Daily Planet building was shaking. It began to fall, and the crowd below screamed. Superman heard the scream and saw the globe falling. Suddenly he was there below it. He caught it and put it down carefully on the street.

Jimmy was there with his camera. *Click. Click. Click.* He took lots of perfect photos of Superman. Perry White walked up to Superman.

'Perry White, *Daily Planet*,' he said. 'What's happening now, Superman? Is it over?'

'No,' said Superman, 'and I need your help. Call the radio stations. Ask them to tell everyone to get out of the buildings. Tell them to go to the city park.'

Superman began to fly.

'Where are you going?' asked Perry.

'If I don't stop this thing soon,' said Superman, 'there won't be a city.'

CHAPTER 12
'Goodbye Superman!'

From his comfortable helicopter, Luthor watched the Atlantic. The crystals were growing fast under the sea, getting higher and higher. Soon they would cut through the sea.

'Goodbye, Miss Lane,' he said.

Lois and Jason fell from side to side in the kitchen, as the yacht shook in the angry sea. Icy water was rising all around them. The lights went off.

'It was wrong to bring Jason with me,' Lois thought.

Then she saw a light above her. A hand appeared and pulled her up.

'Richard! How did you get here?' she asked.

'I flew in the seaplane,' he said. Richard pulled Jason out of the water.

'This is all because of Lex Luthor,' said Lois.

Suddenly the yacht crashed down in the sea.

'Hold on!' shouted Lois.

Lois saw the door beginning to close. She tried to stop it.

'No!' she cried as she fought to reach it. She knew it would be impossible to open from the inside.

'Lois! No!' shouted Richard. 'It's too heavy!'

Too late. The door crashed down and hit Lois. She fell under the water. The water was rising. It was almost at the top of the room.

'We'll die soon,' thought Richard.

Then, suddenly, the door above them was pulled away, and Superman had them in his arms. He carried them to the seaplane.

'You're … him!' said Richard.

'You must be Richard,' said Superman. 'I've heard so much about you.'

'You … have?' said Richard, surprised.

'Is Mom OK?' asked Jason.

Superman listened to Lois's heart. 'She'll be fine,' he said.

'Lois said Lex Luthor has done all this,' said Richard.

'Can you fly out of here?' Superman asked him.

'No, I can't take off in this!' said Richard.

'No problem,' said Superman. 'I'll push. Just promise that you won't come back.'

'I promise,' said Richard.

Superman flew over New Krypton and saw a huge crystal building. Next to it was an empty helicopter. Superman landed beside it.

'Well, hello, old friend,' came a voice. Lex Luthor walked out with Kitty Kowalski.

'Give me my crystal, Luthor,' said Superman. He moved

towards Luthor. Luthor hit him in the face. Superman fell to the ground. He touched his mouth. There was blood. 'What's happening to me?' he thought.

Lois woke up. 'Where am I?' she thought. Then she saw they were in the seaplane.

'How did we get here?' she asked.

'Superman,' said Richard.

'Where is he now?'

'I think he went to stop Luthor.'

'Richard, we must go and help him,' cried Lois. 'There's kyptonite in those crystals. Superman could die!'

'I'm sorry you didn't die on Krypton,' said Luthor, looking down at Superman. 'But you're going to die now. There's kryptonite in these crystals and they will grow everywhere. You can't go back to Krypton and you won't be able to live on Earth.'

Luthor pulled a large piece of kryptonite from his pocket. He raised it high, then pushed it hard into Superman's back. Superman screamed. He moved slowly to the edge of the ice and fell into the sea. Luthor watched him go under the water. He smiled. 'Goodbye, Superman!' he said.

Superman turned round and round as he fell through the water. Crystals were growing towards him from everywhere. And they shone green with kryptonite.

'The crystals are going to kill me,' he thought.

Richard was flying his seaplane towards the island of

tall crystals.

'There he is!' said Jason excitedly.

The plane flew down over the water. Lois jumped in the ocean and swam down to Superman. The crystals were pushing against him. She put her arms around him and pulled and pulled. Finally he was free. Richard helped Lois pull Superman onto the plane.

'Kryptonite …' whispered Superman. 'Back …'

'No, you can't go back,' said Lois.

Richard was trying to get the plane into the sky but there were too many crystals.

'That way, Dad!' said Jason. The plane flew up.

'Mom,' said Jason. 'When Superman said *back*, I think he meant *his* back.' Jason pointed to his own back.

Lois looked. She saw a large piece of kryptonite deep in Superman's back. She pulled it out. There was no blood but his back was black, like a burn. She threw the kryptonite into the sea. Superman opened his eyes.

'You promised you wouldn't come back,' he said to Richard.

'I lied,' Richard smiled.

Superman got up. 'I have to go back,' he said.

'No!' cried Lois. 'You'll die!'

He looked into her eyes. 'Goodbye, Lois,' he said. WHOOSH! He was gone.

CHAPTER 13
Superman saves the world

Only the sun could help Superman now, and he flew up towards it. Below him, New Krypton was growing and growing. Luthor had done a terrible thing.

Superman stayed in the sunlight until he felt completely strong again. Then he flew down. His eyes shone red as he looked at the sea. The sea temperature rose. It became very hot. The bottom of the sea became soft. Superman swam into it. He made a huge hole under Luthor's island. Now he could lift it.

Luthor felt the ground shake. He watched in horror as huge crystals began to fall. One fell on top of Luthor's men.

'Move!' shouted Luthor to Kitty. 'Run to the helicopter!'

They jumped inside the helicopter and Luthor tried to start the engine. They fell into a deep hole and then VROOOM! the engine started. Luthor and Kitty flew up into the sky. Luthor looked back at New Krypton. He saw it rise higher and higher until it was above the ocean.

And below it, pushing it up and up, was Superman.

Lois, Richard and Jason were also watching from their seaplane.

'Wow!' said Jason. 'That's awesome!'

Lois could see that Superman was in trouble. Superman knew he was in trouble too. He tried to move fast. This was the hardest thing he had ever done. Up … up … through the storm clouds.

'I have to hurry,' he thought. 'Higher. Faster.'

Up … up … and out into space. He was getting weaker and weaker. Finally, with difficulty, Superman threw New Krypton towards the sun. The sun would destroy the island. 'It will destroy my special crystal, too,' he thought sadly. He had saved the Earth, but now his connection with Krypton would be lost for ever. He shut his eyes and fell towards Earth.

Superman fell fast towards Metropolis like a star. There was fire all around him. People pointed and watched or screamed and ran. He landed in the city park with a loud explosion, and lay at the bottom of a large hole. A crowd of people looked into the hole.

'It's Superman,' said a policeman. 'He saved the city.'

'Is he dead?' asked a young woman.

'No!' said a boy. 'He's Superman!'

'He was in a hurry to get to Metropolis,' said a man. 'Now he's home.'

'All he needs is a little sunlight,' said an old woman. 'And he'll be fine in the morning.'

The next morning in the Daily Planet office, they were all looking at the front page of the newspaper. SUPERMAN SAVES THE WORLD it said. Next to it was Jimmy's picture of Superman catching the Daily Planet globe.

'Well done, everyone,' said Richard.

Jason ran through the office wearing a red towel. 'I'm Superman!' he shouted. 'I saved the world!'

'Nice article on what Superman did during the earthquake, Clark,' said Lois.

'Thanks,' said Clark.

'But Luthor escaped,' she said. 'I wonder where he went.'

She thought for a moment, then got up. 'I've got an idea,' she said. 'Can you do dinner, Richard? I might be home late.' She walked out of the door.

Richard smiled at Clark. 'I think Luthor's in trouble,' he said.

◈◈◈

Superman flew over Metropolis and saw there was a lot of work to do. He helped builders mend buildings. He flew people with injuries to hospitals. He rescued animals. He carried food to hungry people.

And he was happy. He had saved Metropolis. He had saved the Earth.

And he finally understood what it meant to *belong*. It wasn't about where you came from. It was about what you chose to do. It was about being happy with yourself. And most of all, it was about helping other people.

He would always love Lois. But she belonged to Richard now.

Superman belonged to the city of Metropolis … and the world.

FACT FILE

SUPERMAN: the facts

NAME: Earth name – Clark Kent
Krypton name – Kal-El
Also known as The Man of Steel

BORN: on the planet Krypton

LIVES: in the city of Metropolis, and at the Fortress of Solitude in the Arctic

SPECIAL POWERS:
- Can fly
- Can run at superspeed
- Can jump over high buildings
- Has superstrength: can lift cars and houses
- Can see through things
- Can heat things with his eyes

EQUIPMENT: only his red and blue suit

WEAKNESS: kryptonite takes away his strength. Only the Earth's sun can return it.

ENEMY: Lex Luthor

LOVES: Lois Lane

Superman came to Earth from the planet Krypton. His father, Jor-El, knew there would be an explosion so he put his son Kal-El in a spaceship and sent him to Earth. The spaceship landed in the town of Smallville. The people who found him, Jonathan and Martha Kent, became his Earth parents. They called him Clark. As Clark got older, it became clear that he was very special…

What do these words mean? You can use a dictionary.

power   strength   energy   breathe   gravity   hormones   emergency

The SCIENCE of Superman

Of course, Krypton isn't a real planet, and kryptonite doesn't exist – luckily! But we do know some things about the science behind Superman.

Q: Why is Superman so strong?
A: Superman's strength comes from Earth's yellow sun which gives him his powers. The sun won't give us superstrength, of course, but it gives us life. Plants get all their energy from the sun. This energy is very important to us. It makes food for animals and air to breathe.

Q: What could destroy a planet?

A: If a giant rock crashed into Earth, it would break the planet into bits. Over time, the pieces would come together and make a new planet. This might have one or two large moons. Scientists think Earth's moon was made in this way. If a planet's sun explodes, that planet is destroyed.

Q: Does superstrength really exist?
A: We can never be strong like Superman because of Earth's gravity. It pulls us to the Earth. But when people go the moon, they can do 25 metre jumps and lift big things easily. This is because the moon has much weaker gravity than Earth.

However, sometimes people can do amazing things. For example, in an emergency there are more hormones in the blood. This means that more oxygen (O_2) goes to the body. So sometimes people can lift very heavy things, like cars.

Look at Superman's special powers. What would Superman do?
Clark Kent is at the Daily Planet offices one evening when the phone rings. It's Lois. She sounds terrible. Her son, Jason, is lost. He didn't come home from school. She doesn't know what to do. What does Clark/Superman do?

FACT FILE

Daily Planet
EARTHQUAKE HITS METROPOLIS!

Lex Luthor threw kryptonite into the sea and caused an earthquake that almost destroyed the city of Metropolis. But why do earthquakes usually happen?

Why does the Earth move?

There are twelve main 'tectonic plates' on the Earth. They are always moving, although very slowly. The centre of the Earth is very, very hot. It heats the rock around it to temperatures of over 5000 degrees. The rock is liquid rock.

The tectonic plates sit on top of the liquid rock.

Where two plates meet at a 'fault' (line of weakness) they move against each other. The pressure grows. When the rock between the two plates gets very weak, the ground moves.

Waves travel up to the land above and there is an earthquake.

What do these words mean? You can use a dictionary.
to cause   liquid   pressure   volcano

QUAKES

Children at a school in Japan

Danger areas

Earthquake danger areas are anywhere where plates meet, for example, Japan, Indonesia, western America and the Middle East.

A very small earthquake is called a tremor. Japan has over 1000 tremors a year. Japan is on top of several plates so it is in a very dangerous position. In Japanese schools, children learn what to do in an earthquake. Iran in the Middle East has small earthquakes every day. In December 2003, there was a huge earthquake in the old city of Bam. Over 26,000 people died and almost all the old buildings were destroyed.

Los Angeles, 1994

South-west California in the USA is one of the most well-known earthquake areas in the world. Many earthquakes start in the famous San Andreas Fault. However the last earthquake came from a different fault. It hit Los Angeles in 1994. It lasted 15 seconds but killed 51 people and 22,000 people lost their homes. Scientists don't know when the next big earthquake will happen.

> More people die in earthquakes in poorer countries (e.g. the Middle East) than in richer countries (e.g. Japan, USA). Why do you think this is?
> Would you be afraid to live in an earthquake danger area? Why / Why not?

FACT FILE

21ST CENTURY NEWS

❝ Lois, forget the blackout! You're going to write about Superman! ❞
Life can be difficult at the Daily Planet newspaper. Perry White always seems to be angry. But what's life at a real newspaper like?

THE EDITOR

❝ You live by the headlines, you die by the headlines! ❞

The main editor of a newspaper runs the paper. Every morning they check the news and decide what will make a good story. Then they have a meeting with their reporters and suggest ideas for their articles.

The editor decides which story goes on the front page. They often have to make difficult choices. Politicians, for example, can lose their jobs because of bad headlines and stories. Secrets might sell papers, but the editor has to be sure that the facts are correct – or they could lose their job too!

> ✔ BEST THING:
> No day is the same.
> It's an exciting job.
> ✘ WORST THING:
> Stress, stress and more stress!

THE REPORTER

❝ It's all about the story! ❞

Reporters need to have a good 'nose' for a story. They have to be interested in people and things that are happening in the world. They also need to be determined. Reporters usually have lots of 'sources'. These are people who can give information for new stories.

Sometimes reporters go 'undercover'. They pretend to be someone else to get a good story. In 2003, a reporter from *The Daily Mirror* worked at Buckingham Palace as a footman for two months. When he left he wrote about it. The Queen wasn't very happy!

What do these words mean? You can use a dictionary.
stress determined
footman palace
terrorist

> ✔ BEST THING:
> You meet a lot of people and see different things.
> ✘ WORST THING:
> Reporters can be very unpopular!

THE PHOTOGRAPHER

❝ Today's picture is useless tomorrow! ❞

A newspaper without photos wouldn't sell many copies. A strong photo on the front page will sell the paper. A photographer has to be in the right place at the right time, though. In Superman Returns, Jimmy Olsen finds this difficult!

A good photographer has to be quick-thinking but patient and good with people. They may have to wait a long time for an important politician or famous person to appear. A newspaper often has different photographers for different parts of the paper, for example, sport and travel.

Now, most newspaper photographers use digital cameras. For speed, they often email photos back to the office.

```
    ✔ BEST THING:
The chance to see things
         first!
    ✘ WORST THING:
It's an all weather job!
```

Discuss
1 Imagine you work on a newspaper. What job would you like to do?
2 Do you read any newspapers or magazines? Which one/s? What are your favourite parts?

The right place at the right time!

Perry White:
❝ Jimmy – that photo was taken by a twelve-year-old with a camera phone! Where are our photos?! ❞

Camera phones, video phones, blogs … New technology means that everyone has the chance to be a reporter or photographer now.

On July 7th, 2005, there was a terrorist attack in London. The first photos on TV were sent in by people who were there. They took photos and recorded mini-videos on their mobile phones.

Weblogs or blogs are a very popular way of writing online. Many newspaper websites now have a blog section. Anyone can start a blog. People from all over the world write about their jobs and lives. Newspapers often use people's blogs as ideas for articles.

An unnamed woman from Iraq kept a blog about everyday life during the Iraq war. Her blog is now a book called *Baghdad's Burning: Girl Blog from Iraq*.

SELF-STUDY ACTIVITIES

CHAPTERS 1-5

Before you read

You can use your dictionary for these questions.

1 Which of these words are related to: a) transport b) newspapers?
   article   headline   helicopter   reporter   rocket   spaceship   yacht

2 Complete the sentences with these words.
   award   blackout   Earth   engine   explosion   planet   wig
   a) He had no hair so he wore a ………. .
   b) Halle Berry won the ………. for best actress at the Oscars.
   c) I can't start the car. I think there's a problem with the ………. .
   d) There was a complete ………. . All the lights went out.
   e) The gas was on when she started the fire. There was an ………. .
   f) There are nine ………. around the sun. We live on the ………. .

3 Match the words with their definitions.
   a) baseball   i   to save
   b) a meteorite   ii a small copy of something
   c) to launch   iii a place to watch sport
   d) a model   iv a glass stone
   e) to protect   v   to send off a rocket
   f) a stadium   vi a game
   g) a crystal   vii a large stone from space

After you read

4 Answer the questions.
   a) Why did Superman become Clark Kent?
   b) Why did he go back to Krypton? What happened there? How long was he away?
   c) What did Lois Lane say in her article 'Why the world doesn't need Superman'? Was it a good article? How do you know?
   d) Where did Lex Luthor go in his yacht? What did he do there?
   e) Why was there a blackout in Metropolis?
   f) What happened to the plane with the rocket on it? How did Superman save it?

5 What do you think?
   a) Is Superman still in love with Lois Lane? Is she in love with him?
   b) Is Lois right when she says that the world doesn't need Superman?

CHAPTERS 6-9

Before you read

You can use you dictionary for these questions.

6 Circle all the words which are parts of a car.

**brakes   wheels   engine   mirror   lights   launcher
stone   windows   doors   heart   wig   award**

7 What's going to happen next? Have a guess!
   a) What are Lex Luthor and his friends planning to do? Will they be successful?
   b) What will happen to the friendship between Lois and Superman? And between Lois and Clark Kent?

After you read

8 Are these sentences true or false? Correct the false sentences.
   a) Superman decided to help people again and he helped people all over the world.
   b) Luthor stole a meteorite with kryptonite inside it from a museum.
   c) Lois was happy when Perry told her to write about Superman because she wanted to interview him.
   d) Kitty pretended that the brakes on her car weren't working.
   e) Luthor took a piece of kryptonite from the meteorite and put it in his pocket.
   f) Lois doesn't think the blackout story is more important than writing about Superman.
   g) When Superman flew to the Fortress of Solitude in the Arctic, everything was the same as usual.

9 What do you think?
   a) What will happen to Lois and Jason on the yacht?
   b) Will Luthor's plan work?
   c) Will Luthor kill Superman?

SELF-STUDY ACTIVITIES

CHAPTERS 10-13

Before you read

You can use a dictionary for these questions.

10 Answer the questions.
   a) Which of these can make a loud noise?
   **engine   helicopter   explosion   earthquake
   rocket   wig   yacht   brake**
   b) Which of these are round?
   earth   planet   headline   globe   meteorite   baseball
   c) Which of these are people?
   farmer   reporter   launcher   protector

11 What's going to happen next? Have a guess!
   a) Will Superman be able to stop Luthor? If so, how?
   b) What's the most dangerous thing for Superman? How will he be able to survive?
   c) Will Jimmy Olsen get a good photograph of Superman?
   d) Will Superman tell Lois who he really is?

After you read

12 Complete the sentences with the correct names. You can use the names more than once.
   Superman   Lois   Luthor   Jimmy   Richard
   a) .... launched a rocket carrying kryptonite and the large crystal into the sea.
   b) .... tried to send a fax with the position of the yacht.
   c) .... took lots of photos of Superman as he caught the huge globe.
   d) .... tried to rescue Lois and Jason, but the door shut.
   e) .... tried to kill Superman by hitting him in the back with a piece of kryptonite.
   f) .... pulled the kryptonite out of Superman's back.
   g) .... got his strength back from the sun and then heated the sea with his eyes.

13 What do you think?
   a) Do you like the way the story ends? If you could write a different ending, what would it be?
   b) What will happen to Lois, Jason and Richard in the future?
   c) Will Lois find Luthor? If so, what will happen?